Immanuel

by Seth Rubio

PublishAmerica
Baltimore

First printing

At the specific preference of the author, PublishAmerica allowed this work to remain exactly as the author intended, verbatim, without editorial input.

ISBN: 1-4241-2049-7
PUBLISHED BY PUBLISHAMERICA, LLLP
www.publishamerica.com
Baltimore

Printed in the United States of America

Acknowledgements

Though this very book is written to expound on this acknowledgement and at the risk of sounding trite, I would like to give all honor and praise to my amazing Lord and Savior, Jesus Christ. For truly, Lord, You are my very life, my breath of fresh air in the heat of summer, my warm blanket in the dead of winter. Thank You for loving me in my sin and for capturing me with the unparalleled beauty of Your face. Father, I love You for Who you are as the Eternal Almighty God, Creator of heaven and earth, Sustainer of my life. Holy Spirit, thank You for filling me to overflowing with the divine love of my wonderful Christ and for leading me always beside still waters. I owe all that I am and all that I have to you, my Lord and my God!

I would also like to acknowledge my wonderful family, who through great sacrifice and love have helped to make this book possible. Without your love and support, I would not be the man I am today, nor would the writings adorning the pages of this book be in existence. Mom and Dad, simply stated, you will never know how much you mean to me. I cannot imagine any set of parents displaying with more accuracy the unconditional love of the Lord before their children than you have before your three boys. Greg and David, you are true men of God, whose lives have touched me in ways I may not comprehend until heaven. Thank you for being such Godly husbands, fathers, and brothers. Your stalwart lives have and will always serve as a wonderful example for me. A family like mine makes the task of seeing clearly the love and life of Christ a much easier one. Thank you.

Introduction

Though diverse in nature, every one of these writings has as its foundation the life changing truth that God became a Man and "dwelt among us", hence the title, Immanuel ("God with us"). Whether prose or poetry, each one was written with the same intention: to draw the reader (you) as well as the author (me) into a deeper relationship with our great God and Savior Jesus Christ. "How were you writing to yourself?", you ask. Good question, and the answer provides a nice segue into my motivation for writing the book, so thank you for asking. The answer is as follows: I would venture to say that I have gained as much out of writing these vignettes as any reader of them may gain. Just as is the case with any blood-bought Jesus person, I am in great need of His touch and His grace. Well, in His great mercy, the Lord really ministered to me through these writings, and I pray that after reading these, you will have a similar testimony. For these excerpts were born not out of a perfect man's desire to teach the world a thing or two about God. On the contrary, they were born out an imperfect man's desire to share with other imperfect people about a Perfect God Who loved him with fierce, unending love and offers the same love to them!

Each writing stemmed from my meditation upon the Lord or upon His Word. As I would ponder the Lord or read a Scripture, He would allow me to catch a peek of a certain facet of His Being. He would then give me words to express this facet, although, as one of the writings denotes, there are no words to adequately convey the greatness of our amazing God! The Lord has been so good to expand my vision and experience of Him through this time of writing, and my deep desire is for Him *alone* to be glorified. And whether you are a long-time lover of the Lord Jesus or you are unsaved and simply curious, my prayer is the same: "Lord God, anoint the words upon these pages with the Presence of Your Holy Spirit. Allow the readers to experience the unrivaled touch of the Living God as they move through the pages of this book. Whether saved or not, may they be drawn to the One Who formed them and loves them with everlasting love. May the eyes of their hearts be opened to behold Your glory and the ears of their hearts be attuned to Your sweet voice. Father, infuse them with deep revelation of Your glorious Son, Jesus the Christ. You are worthy of all honor and praise, Eternal One, and I give thanks unto Your Name for Your unending love. Come Lord Jesus! Amen."

God in Flesh

God in flesh—this Baby Boy,
so gently lying there.
His Life so tender yet so strong,
all my sin to bear.

For me this God became a Man-
O how can it be true?
That Love Divine should take on skin
and die for me and you!

The One Who spoke and stars were formed
is so in love with me
that thinking not of His own Life,
He hung upon a tree.

Alive again, He looks my way
and gently calls my name.
"Yes, Lord, my God, You gave Your all;
now I shall do the same."

Mark 4:39

In this time of uncertainty, as the winds and waves of life ferociously beat against you from every side, may you experience the limitless power of Christ's love as He whispers, "Peace, be still", thrusting you into the depths of His divine rest. May His heart that beats for you quicken your inner being, shattering all fear and doubt and infusing you with hope that sustains. For the Lord our God is a God replete with divine power to meet every need you have and to defeat every obstacle you face. So see Him amid the storm lifting His holy hand, and hear the echo of His voice so strong as He calms the storm as well as your heart.

John 11:17-44

Tears that pour like rain from a battered and torn soul are as incense before the Lord our God. He wept with those who wept as He neared the tomb of Lazarus, knowing only moments later He would raise him from the dead. His is a love beyond compare—a love without end. His is a love that weeps with ruthless compassion then moves Him to raise the dead. May your tears rise before Him as incense, moving Him to tears of compassion, resulting in resurrection life.

Revelation 1:14

Through the night of endless pain, beyond the depths of deepest sorrow, there is a Man who lives to save. His blazing eyes of fire burn to love you and His heart so full of passion beats to hold you. This Man so strong and kind stripped Himself of all dignity and stretched His perfect and bloodied body across all ages. He did this so that you might be pierced by those fiery eyes and captured by that passionate heart. So in the midst of your pain and grief that violently strangle hope, simply gaze into the eyes of the Lord your God and be swept off your feet by His heart that beats for you.

Hebrews 12:2

O, to bask in the Presence of the Lord Jesus Christ! To dwell in the radiant glory of His love! For this you were created; to this end you must give your all. To live for less is to cheapen that precious blood that was shed at Calvary. For it has been said that it was the "joy that was set before Him" that compelled Him to endure the Cross. This joy set forth before our Lord was the day your sin no longer hindered Him from being with you. "O, that you would venture beyond the outer and inner courts and even the Holy Place!" He beckons. "I have paid the price. The veil has been rent asunder. Come, my bride! I long for intimacy with you in the Holy of Holies!" Do you hear His still small voice wooing and winning your heart? He alone, as the Lover of your soul, satisfies fully. Let yourself be lost in Him today, and in so doing, truly be found at last!

Jeremiah 31:3

"Grieve not, my child," says the Lord your God. "I love you with an everlasting love! I love you with an unconditional love! I died and rose again that I might lavish this love upon you, my child. Simply open the floodgates of your heart and allow the tidal wave of my love for you to wash away all your pain. For as my power and glory are without end, so is my pure and unadulterated love for you, my precious one. I long to hold you in my arms and whisper to you in the night. Let me be your hope and your stay in this difficult time. Allow me to consume those places of pain in your heart with the blazing fire of my love. You have nothing to fear, for I am your Everlasting Father and I love you with an everlasting love!"

Triune God

Great Father, my King, Creator of all,
You alone are the God before Whom I fall!
Designer of life, to Your grace I run.
With Your holy love, expressed through Your Son,
consume now my heart! May Your will be done!

Jesus my Lord, so pure and so strong,
my heart have you captured and given a song!
This song you have birthed so deep in my soul
tells how Your sweet grace and mercy did roll
my burden away, and then made me whole!

O Holy Ghost, breathe deep within me
sweet mercies of God, my soul to set free!
Spirit of Truth, of Life, and of Love,
touch now my heart. Descend like a dove,
and fill me with God's holy peace from above!

Father of lights, sweet Spirit, and Son,
equal in pow'r, You reign—Three in One!
Sufficiently strong, You meet every need.
My thirst, how You quench! My hunger You feed!
And, saving my soul, Your Body did bleed!

Luke 7:50

O, my soul longs for the God whose Name is above all others! The beautiful God-Man they call "the friend of sinners" is the desire of my heart. Have you met this Jesus of Nazareth? He looks at me and loves me, despite my many failings. My weary soul pours rivers of tears upon His nail-pierced feet, and He cleanses me with the word from His divinely sweet lips: "Your faith has saved you; go in peace." O, to plunge into the depths of this ocean of love! You must fall at the feet of this God and allow His love to conquer you. O, to be conquered by this God so full of love and grace! This is why you were born. You must know this Lover of your soul, for He died that you might live.

Zephaniah 3:17

My heart is a fountain of your Love, O my Lord. May the flow of Your rushing waters be ever unimpeded and daily increasing as You form Yourself in the depths of my soul. I long to radiate the emanating light of Your goodness and glory in a world bereft of hope. I live to dance with You, O Lover of my soul, to the song that brought my heart to life when first we met. For You sang over me a love song whose melody is the beating of Your heart for Your child-Your bride. With one lyric of Your love song You quiet my soul yet cause it to erupt. Yes, my Lover-King, You have captured my heart for eternity. May my life be the mouthpiece through which You sing over others this life-giving lyric, O my Lord, inviting them to true life!

The Greatest Miracle

God Almighty could become a Man. Herein abides not only a mystery beyond the mind's comprehension, but also evidence of a power greater than any ever before known. That God could become a man denotes a power beyond compare. For unspeakably mighty is the power that can cause the One who is uncontainable to be housed in flesh. And yet, as amazing as this miracle is, it is not the greatest. For an even greater miracle is the Love that compelled Him to perform such a feat. The single greatest miracle in all of creation is not that God *could* become a Man, but that God *would* become a Man. Looking upon the mass of depravity dubbed "humanity", this awesome God who owed no one anything, self-existent in Nature, loved us. When He had every right to destroy us or, at the very least, to leave us to our own inevitable self-destruction, He simply loved us instead. He so passionately loved us, in fact, that He did indeed become a Man. Knowing that He was our only hope, this Jesus Christ, King of the universe, traded His kingly robe of Heaven for the swaddling clothes of a baby and fully entered in to the human mess in order to set things right. With a manger for His bed, our God forever put to rest any argument that He is a distant God Who cannot relate to us as humans. He had no grand entrance into this earth. On the contrary, the Lord of Hosts had only a peasant couple and some barn animals for His welcoming committee. Furthermore, He was not born in a luxurious palace as would be expected for Someone of royal descent. Rather, the King of Glory was born in a smelly stable. This is the God whom we serve, a God so full of compassion that He humbled Himself to a place equal to that of "the least of these"! However, this infant lying in a manger was anything but normal, for awaiting Him was a destiny that was to include His eternal redemption of a lost and broken humanity! This God of Heaven became a flesh and blood Man and in the process displayed a Love that stands forever as the greatest miracle of all.

Isaiah 40:26

Who speaks stars into existence and calls them each by name? He is the Lord your God. Who with the breath of His mouth and the brightness of His appearing destroys His enemies? He is the Lord your God. Who calms the storm and raises the dead with but a word? He is the Lord your God. And this God over all other gods waits on high to show compassion to you! His heart is aflame with desire for you, O burdened soul. In exchange for your burden, He longs to impart to you His unceasing reservoir of strength and power. He is raging with fiery passion for you, O beautiful bride of Christ. Allow Him to consume the dross of your life with the bonfire of His relentless love—yes even to flow this love through the very pores of your life to others! He waits to explode His unending Life in and through you. Yield today unto this God, for He is the Lord your God!

Psalm 24:7

In the Lord of Hosts I place my eternal trust, for You alone, O Lord, are the Rock. As You are ever strong and only good, I waver not to release fully the deepest treasures of my heart to You, my King. I unreservedly fling open the doors of my soul to you, O my God, and I invite You to flood my being with the matchless beauty and glory of Your Presence! O reign in me in Your fullness, dearest Jesus! May the life that I live be defined by the very essence of Who You are! O, wonder of wonders—that You, my God, would transform my folly into Your holiness! Yes, Lord! My soul yearns to cry unto the Lord my God, "I am yours and You are mine, O Lord!"

Newness of Life

Your rhythms of love awaken my soul,
to newness of life divine!
Inhaling Your winds of mercy so rich,
I own this love as mine!

Your hands have clothed me in garb of grace,
replacing rags with glory!
Of such a grace I ne'er have dreamt,
My life must tell its story!

Your breath in me consumes my heart
with zeal for You, my Lord!
By holy fire and healing love,
my life you have restored!

Your cross forever my hope and joy,
I live to hold it high!
That others may open their lives to you,
to myself, I shall die!

I Corinthians 15:54-55

"Where, O death, is your victory?" says the Lord God Almighty. "Where, O death, is your sting? Am I not the God over all creation? Do I not reign in majesty above all that the eye may and may not see? My Son has been highly exalted, having divinely conquered you through His cross at Calvary. For His obedience to you was but a means to an O so glorious end: His eternal victory over you. Risen from the dead, He has forever received the Name above all names, that before this Name-the Name of Jesus-every knee in heaven above and on earth below shall humbly bow. And you, O ruthless murderer of life, are by no means exempt from this decree. For indeed you have at last and for all time been defeated by the love of this Christ. Now, having been swallowed up in My glorious victory, you continue on, serving as a mere segue from life unto Life for those covered by the precious blood of my Son."

Psalm 18

Gripping my heart with claws of fear, my enemy goes for the kill. It seems as though my life is flashing before my very eyes. Hopeless and despairing, I hold on by a thread for dear life. "Dear Jesus, please save me…" are the fading words forced from heart through lips. And then, as a bolt of lightning streaks across the sky without warning, so this Rider comes forth from Heaven's throne. He appears in a blaze of glory and does with one breath defeat my adversary. He rescues me and lifts me to ride upon His brilliantly white steed. "Fear not, my son. For once though lost, you now are found. And with Me you will ride for eternity, as I reveal to you the depths of Me. The life you lived in your own power for your own sake and to your own end has forever ceased. The Life that I now birth in You is altogether different than you've known before. Your new life is to be lived in my power for My sake and to My glorious end. And though the Ride I take you on is fraught with twists and turns, my love for you will be forever Your overflowing source of courage. I love you, my child, and I rescued you so that I might make you one with Me. So always and only in Me abide, forsaking all others. And you will know the joy sublime, the Ride above all rides."

Surrender

Ever present, ageless God—there is none like You. Radiant in majesty, full of splendor—You shine forth in glory, driving the stars to their knees. O, my awesome Lord, who am I that You would beckon me to Your side? Who am I that the Creator of all would long to sup with me? And yet I hear You call in that still small voice—You so tenderly whisper my name. So I run to You, my Lord and King, for You are my Beginning and End. And as You supremely reign in the heavens above, may You also find in my heart a throne fit just for You.

Home Sweet Home

If ever your heart is wandering far from its home in the Lord your God, know this, precious child of the King: remaining steadfastly true, His heart for you beats ever strong. He is overflowing with compassion and waits on high to lavish it upon you. So in that moment, as you feel the weight of guilt and fear pressing down hard, simply turn your eyes to your blessed Savior and be captured anew by His relentless love. For in the time it takes you to say, "I'm sorry", Jesus lifts you with His everlasting arms of love and restores you to your home in Him.

Life in the Lord

To live in the Lord is to rest in His love.
To rest in His love is to rise in His strength.
To rise in His strength is to stand in His peace.
To stand in His peace is to walk in His joy.
To walk in His joy is to run in His race.
To run in His race is to soar in His grace.

Lord, in all I do, may my life ever be found in You.

Isaiah 40:31

When on this pilgrim journey you feel you cannot press onward, rest, weary traveler, in the arms of the Lord your God. He knows the road is long and the way difficult, for He traveled the same path. Divesting Himself of His glory, He took on flesh and walked as one of us so that He might relate fully to His own. Now, having successfully completed His journey by conquering death, He reigns on high and waits to show compassion to you. Allow this seasoned Veteran—this wonderful God—to catch you up into His arms of love. Allow His divine strength to consume your very being, causing you fly as the eagle flies. For He says to you, "Rest in me, child, and discover that my Presence will carry you victoriously to the end."

Father's Purpose

As I gaze upon Your broken body
hanging on that tree,
I marvel at this awesome love;
why would you die for me?

For what in heav'n or on the earth
is truly worthy of
this blood so rich, so sweet, so pure,
this God so full of love?

I see my sin; I feel my shame.
I can bear this pain no more.
Knowing that this sin of mine
has crucified the Lord!

And now—what's this? My Jesus Christ!
You're risen from the dead!
This Lamb once slain and buried deep
is now lifting up my head!

"My child," You say with tender voice
as you wipe away my tears.
"Please allow my perfect love
to cast out all your fears.

My death upon that rugged cross
had at its bloody end
the purpose of my Father's heart,
too deep to comprehend.

O wonder of wonders—mystery of ages—
But yes, O yes, it's true!
This purpose of my Father was
that I should die for you.

And in so doing purchase her—
My pure and spotless bride.
So walk with me and talk with me;
always in me abide.

For on this day that's called 'Today'
I've won the victory.
Now you are Mine and I am yours
for all eternity."

God's Perspective

As winter frost announces the arrival of a bleak season, may our eyes and ears be attentive to the Lord. For He would have us to live out of His heavenly perspective rather than out of an earthly one. When the natural man wants to go the way of the pessimist and attempt to simply endure, the spirit man must rise up and be "more than a conqueror"! The winter season is one in which the Lord desires to bring a deeper revelation of His Son's "bleak season" on the cross and the victory for us that resides therein. For on that cross, our Lord died to wash away our sins through the power of His precious blood. Furthermore, He died to free us from the power of sin over our lives, that we may walk in His holiness! Hallelujah! Yes, during history's darkest hour, as all creation trembled at the death of its Master, the greatest victory was won as Jesus Christ redeemed mankind! So in the hour that seems so bleak, let us tune our ears to hear His words, "as winter is a necessary means to a glorious spring, so is death a doorway unto Life."

Acts 16:25

As I sit here in this prison cell, the questions perpetually flood my mind. For I know that the Lord has chosen me, set me apart from birth. I am persuaded that He has a great plan for my life. He has promised me an abundant life—one in which He will prosper me and use me for His Kingdom purposes. So how do I now find myself in this dingy prison cell whose only view is that of the criminals of society? How am I to live the abundant, prosperous life if I am bound up in these chains? How is the Lord to use me to minister to His flock from within the tiny confines of these four walls? Though I know not the answers to these questions, I shall rise up in the midst of adversity to praise my God! For Jesus Christ is worthy of my praise at all times, no matter the circumstances. "So here is my heart, O Lord my God! I offer it to you without reservation. I lift my hands, my heart, my life to you, O King Eternal. May this sacrifice of praise rise before You as a sweet aroma and bring a smile to Your beautiful face. Though I do not understand why I am in this prison cell, yet will I rejoice in you and sing a new song to you, my God and Father. Praise and glory be to Your Name! For You have granted me an honor far beyond what I deserve—that I should be afforded the privilege of worshiping You in the midst of adversity! O glorious Potter, please capture this earthen vessel once again and recreate me through fiery trial. Please allow the alabaster box that is my flesh to be broken through this difficulty in order that the perfume of my life—

Your Spirit in me—might escape, permeating the atmosphere and serving as a throne upon which You may sit. Yes, Lord, I surrender to You in this midnight hour and invite You to have Your perfect way in and through me!" And then, in His still small voice, the Lord responds, "I have indeed heard and received your heart's cry, my son. The lesson you have learned in this trial is invaluable: when doubts and fears torment, simply set your gaze upon Me in worship and discover that your prison can become your sanctuary. For true freedom is realized when you use your adversity as a springboard and dive headlong into the depths of all that I AM."

Matthew 8:27

What manner of Man is this?
With but a word He silences storms,
their wrath tamed by His command.

What manner of Man is this?
With but a touch He heals the sick,
their afflictions conquered by His hand.

What manner of Man is this?
With but a glance He steals my heart,
its walls demolished by Love Divine.

What Manner of Man is this?
With but a cross He saves my soul,
making forgiveness in Him forever mine.

Gethsemane

His divine body pouring drops of blood for sweat, our Lord Jesus Christ experienced what was perhaps the most difficult test of His passion in a quaint little garden the night prior to His death. Knowing fully Who He was and what He had come to do, Jesus expressed the depths of His human vulnerability as He pleaded with His Father to deliver Him from the cursed cup being offered to Him. Thrusting Himself, however, upon the will of Father, this faithful High Priest surrendered Himself completely, setting in motion the turn of events that would ultimately climax in His consummate victory over Satan and his offspring, sin and death. That night in Gethsemane was much more than simply a nice story to tell as a precursor to the cross. On the contrary, it was the defining moment in the history of mankind, a moment when the redemption of the human race was literally hanging in the balance. For that well known statement uttered from our Lord's lips, "Father, if it be possible, let this cup pass from Me," was much more than mere lip service given to serve as a filler in a script. Rather, it was the desperate plea of a Man Who simply could not bear the thought of being separated from His Abba Father. Accordingly, His statement of surrender to the Father's will, "yet not my will, but Yours be done" is to be recognized for what it truly is, a throwing of Himself upon the ultimate will of His Father's heart despite His own reservations. So when we are bombarded with fears and anxieties, let us follow in the footsteps of our

Master, Jesus Christ, and fully surrender to the will of our Father. For just as Jesus, having done so, proceeded to fully accomplish His Father's perfect plan, so will we through our total surrender experience the fullness of what God has planned for our lives.

Simply Come

When you feel that your sins have thrust you beyond that dreaded point of no return, and that you have exhausted the Lord's resources of mercy, fear not, treasured child of the Living God! The blood that He shed on that cross so long ago bids you to come. For He knew every sin that you would commit, whether in thought, word, or deed. But this knowledge could not bar the way between Him and you. This He would not allow, for His love and desire for you are far too great! So He went to the cross, fully aware of every one of your shortcomings and failures and sins. Now alive from the dead, this gracious Savior, Jesus the Nazarene, beckons you to fall at His feet in humble repentance so that He may lift you up off the floor and walk hand in hand with you throughout all eternity. Your intimacy with Him depends not upon your perfection, for He has already paid the price so that you might walk clothed in *His* righteousness. Rather, it depends upon your willingness to fully embrace His inexhaustible mercy as He continually offers it to you. For in this embrace is found not only restoration of fellowship with your God, but also the power to live the victoriously abundant Life He has in store for you.

Fly with Christ

Deeper than the deepest ocean and higher than the highest mountain is the Lord's love for you. Riding upon the wings of the wind, this majestic God soars throughout the heavens in anticipation of your cry, tender child of God. He waits on high to rescue you and to catch you up into His divinely strong arms so that He may carry you off into the glorious sunset that is His perfect destiny for you. "Look unto Jesus, the Author and Finisher of your faith," is His Word to you in this moment. Strive no longer to bear the burdens of this life alone, for such is a dead end path. Rather, lift your eyes "unto the hills" and behold the Lord as He rejoices over you with singing. Open wide the gates of your soul and allow His song to infuse you with strength to run the race. For the strength that He imparts to you is a well that never runs dry. On the contrary, you will find that the well only deepens and widens as you partake of its richness. So cast aside hindrance, soldier of the Lord, and fly with Christ your King into the eternal Life that is found in Him!

Fiery Love

I have a passion raging within my heart
to release the Love that consumes like fire.
To hold it in is to quench its holy fury;
through its release are its embers kindled.

Blaze, fire of God! Burn with Love's cry!
My body as your sacrifice, consume my heart!
Lord, may Your Spirit of life and of love
ever live and love through me.

Conquering Love

Hanging between Heaven and earth, Jesus the Savior bleeds sweet drops of divine love. With fiery compassion adorned in tears of agony, His eyes pierce my very soul. They bespeak the unquenchable love that consumes his heart—a love directed toward one such as I! Without uttering a word, He looks at me from that cursed tree and tells me the story of His unending love for me. He silently yet unmistakably speaks to me of my great need and His great desire and ability to meet that need. As earth shakes and Heaven weeps, my heart follows suit, for never before have I encountered such a violent love as the one I see before me. This is no fair weather love; this is no lip service love. Rather, this is radical, passionate, relentless Love whose only limits are those placed upon it by the recipient of it. "Flow, precious Blood of Christ! Flow so purely and powerfully over me, cleansing me of all that is not of my Lord! Savior, Your boundless Love has captured this wandering heart. May this Love forever be the wings of my life upon which I soar with You though the heavens. You have conquered me, mighty and gentle King, and I long for You now to live Your eternal Life through me!"

Love's Desire

As the sun rising in the eastern sky breaks forth in glorious day, so the Lord appears in His splendor. The radiance of His glory emanates from His majestic Body for all to behold. Ablaze with Love's desire, His eyes search throughout the earth for those hearts that are yearning for Him. Yes, He is love sick for His bride, as she is His very highest purpose and the reason He gave His life upon a cross. And she is the passion in His heart that compels Him to employ any and every means in order to attain His desired end: forming her into a bride without spot or wrinkle. For He knows that her true fulfillment resides therein, as her purity gives way to the deep intimacy with Him for which she was created. May His heart find sweetest delight in the utter surrender of this sought after bride, as we give ourselves without reservation to our King! For we are the central and ultimate purpose of this awesome God, and we must fully yield to Him, that He might lay claim to what He purchased on the cross—a glorious bride!

Father's Voice

In the stillness of the night, when fears and doubts surround and you feel helpless to combat them, know that your Creator stands ready to deliver you. The tone of His sweet voice will silence the voice of the enemy. Can you hear Him singing a love song over you? Your heart was created for the very purpose of resting peacefully in the embrace of His song. Find your refuge, child of God, in the arms of Christ, for He is strong to save you. Strive no longer to fight the voices that attack so relentlessly; rather, allow your ears to be attuned to the frequency of your Father's voice. For in the melodies of His love song you will discover deliverance from your foe and peace beyond understanding.

Cross of Christ

As Jesus remains suspended between Heaven and earth, hanging upon this cross, the pain is nearly too much to bear. Still fresh in His mind are His Father's words to Him as He lay down His royal garments and prepared to replace it with that of an infant human, "Always remember that, as a Human, You must remain in constant communion with Me. I love You, My Son." "O, Father, where are You now? Why have You forsaken Me?" is His cry upon the cross. He can feel His physical senses waning as His sense of agony only increases. The physical pain, great though it is, does not compare to the spiritual pain. Deception, lust, hatred, and murder are but a taste of this horrendous onslaught He endures. The weight of all the ages rests upon His shoulders, and He must bear such a load alone, as Father has turned His face away! Yet, He is resolute that He will steadfastly and completely finish the task set before Him. For it is Father's Love that compelled Him to offer His Son as a Sacrifice, and Christ has willingly surrendered the will of His Humanity to the will of Father's Love. And though the horror of this cross is nearly unbearable, it does not compare with the horror of seeing His dear ones lost in their sin forever. For His heart's deepest longing is to reconcile these precious and helpless creatures to their Father, that in Christ they might become the very righteousness of God…"It is finished!"

The Fountain

Are you parched with agonizing thirst?
Come to the Fountain.
Does your soul long for cool refreshment?
Come to the Fountain.

Free and pure is this Fountain's flow,
welcoming all who would come.
A Well so rich and so full,
its depths are far beyond tracing out.
The Lord is an ever-flowing Fountain
gushing forth living water.
Would you drink freely of His Life
every longing and thirst to quench?

John 20:10-16

To hear the Lord of glory call you by name is to be quickened in the Spirit, for an intimate knowledge of the Creator brings forth Life. As Mary wept at the empty tomb of the Lord Jesus, she recognized Him not, even as He stood near to her. In her overwhelming grief, she failed to see the very One over whom she so deeply grieved. But when the Lord called her name, "Mary", she was immediately thrust into the joy of His Presence, for she had an intimate relationship with her Lord. As you grieve in the midst of a trial that seems to be draining you of vitality, may you hear the voice of your Lord as He sweetly calls you by name. For the intimate tone with which He so tenderly calls will surely infuse your very being with joy unspeakable and hope eternal.

God's Love

Filled to overflowing in Your intoxicating Presence, my heart beats with Your love, Lord Jesus Christ! To sup with you, my King and Savior, is the highest end of eternity. For in Your Presence, O Lord, is the fulfillment for which I was created. I long to know You, Lord God of all creation, as You are my very reason for living. That You would lay down Your Divine Life for me is a mystery beyond my mind's conception and worth my life's dedication. Lord, Your tender mercy has eternally captured my lovesick heart. Sweeping me off my feet, You have set at rest for all time any wayward desires of my heart. For what could ever compare with the bliss of basking in Your unconditional love! Your sweet touch is as a cool breeze in the sweltering summer heat, satisfying to the uttermost. Your beauty and glory cause my heart to swell with anticipation of unadulterated intimacy with You. The pores of my life breathe in Your essence, empowering my every weakness and quenching my every thirst. Now may this love that You have so graciously shed abroad in my heart be as boldly evident through my life as it is deeply felt in my heart, beautiful God, that others may be drawn to You. For such is Your love, Father, ever beckoning and ever wooing the hearts of Your precious ones.

John 10:10

Fullness of life is available to you, wandering soul, if you will but open up your heart to the Lord Jesus. Standing at the threshold of your heart's door, He tenderly knocks. Do you hear the melody of the song He sings over you, wooing you to Life Abundant? He knows the emptiness and the pain that threaten to steal the last traces of hope remaining inside your heart. He weeps with you in your agonizing struggle against a faceless foe that relentlessly attempts to eradicate all resolve to go on. And He longs to reach forth His nail-pierced hand into the depths of your being to touch you deeply, that you might be permeated with His love. Through a divine paradox wrought upon Calvary's cross, He desires to impart to you His peace beyond measure and life without end in exchange for your sin and shame. Simply thrust yourself upon the mercy of this awesome God, flinging wide the doors of your life to His lordship and salvation. Having done so, you will experience a divine love that knows no bounds and the fullness of life for which you were created.

Holy Spirit

Holy Spirit, flow through me as a river so pure, washing me in the renewing waters of Christ. Cleanse me of all that is impeding the beauty of Jesus from shining through the portals my life. Lord, I offer my body to You as a vessel through which You may pour Your power and Your glory. Indwelling Spirit of the Living God, consecrate my life unto Father's holy purpose and mold me in the likeness of the Holy Child Jesus. My eyes are Yours; may they ever look away from self and unto the King. My ears are Yours; may they ever be attuned to the Master's sweet voice. My hands are Yours; may they ever cast aside hindrance and take up a cross. My feet are yours; may they ever flee from sin and run Your race. My life is Yours; may it ever reflect the love and grace that my Lord has so richly lavished upon me, to the eternal glory of my great God and King.

Can I Soar?

Can I soar with You, my God, beyond the skies?
O, how Your wings of glory fly me as a kite!
Can I soar with You to the edge of what I've known?
For in You my spirit finds its rest and its flight!

Can I dive with You, Lord God, into the depths?
O, to plumb the ravines of Your wildly beating heart!
Can I feel the exhilarating rush of your breath in me?
You move my soul to a realm in which we ne'er shall part!

Can I scale the wall of Your unfolding glory, my God?
O, that I might catch a glimpse of Your raw splendor!
Can I gaze past the veil of the absolute majesty that is You?
I dare to press upward, that I might behold this God so tender!

Can I lose myself, Lord God, in the wonder of Your love?
O, to be raptured into the unspeakable joy of Heaven's sound!
Can I revel in thoughts of a Day known only by You?
For on that Day I lose myself in You, forever to be found!

Hidden Treasure

Shall I hide in the recesses of my heart this wonderful treasure?
Have I not reason enough to hold it forth for all to see?
For this God so full of love has filled me with His pleasure!
He has promised forever to catch me up into His glory.

Therefore, I must openly impart this treasure to those in need.
His love will I share liberally with those He died to save.
For salvation, though free for me, demanded that He bleed.
Moved with divine compassion, His precious Life He gave.

Lord, here I stand, fully and freely forgiven, clothed in Your grace.
Pardon my hesitancy to extend this treasure to the lost.
I humbly commit to You, my King, the remainder of my days.
Let your love shine through my life, no matter to me the cost.

Look Away

When life overwhelms you with many a burden,
look away unto Jesus the Christ.

When temptation threatens your will to dominate,
look away unto Jesus the Christ.

When guilt strangles last vestiges of hope inside,
Look away unto Jesus the Christ.

He reigns on high in glorious victory,
Awaiting you with sweet mercy and saving love.
So look unto Him in this moment,
And see His grace freely flowing down from above.

Divine Reversal

Lord, when all is well in my life, I rejoice, giving you the praise and the glory for wonderful blessings. And rightfully so, for You are the Giver of all good gifts. When all is going awry in my life, difficulty and trial abounding, I cry out to you for rescue from the struggle. And certainly You are the One upon whom I should call for deliverance. But I long to experience a deeper place in You, my Lord. For there is a place in which a divine reversal is wrought by Your grace, whereby I rejoice in times of difficulty and cry out in times of comfort. O, that my rejoicing would be born out of the place of tribulation! "Count it all joy when you face trials of many kinds," You said in Your Word. Train my heart to sing the song of joy whose melody is the fiery trial that brings forth Spirit-breathed transformation and whose lyrics are the story You are writing in my life. Train my hands to lift Heavenward in praise of You in the midst of difficulty, as such is the welcome mat for Your sanctifying work. And when all is well, let my cry be one of desire for protection from the blessing that leads to stagnation. Keep me from the place of comfort that displaces growth in You. In the end, Lord God, teach me to live in the Spirit at all times, thrusting me into the center of your pleasing and perfect will!

Isaiah 6:1-8

With matchless glory, the Lord of Hosts radiates waves of beauty in His temple. Cries of "Holy!" come forth from winged creatures who serve Him. Their echoes of worship shake the very foundations of the temple, as smoke permeates the place. Highly exalted, the Lord sits upon His glorious throne, and the train of His robe fills the room. As I behold unspeakable glory, I am overwhelmed by the reality of my sin in light of His holiness. Images of past failures relentlessly bombard my mind, giving way to thoughts of what is surely inevitable punishment. "Woe is me! I am unclean! I have beheld the very glory of God!" Bracing for the worst, I am amazed that instead of being consumed by the furious anger of God, I am cleansed by His furious love! He touches me with his fire, burning away all dross and sin, and in so doing captures my heart forever. His words are as music to my ears, "Whom shall I send? And who will go for us?" With excitement cloaked in humility, I reply, "Here am I. Send me!" That this God so full of majesty would accept me-yea, use me-is beyond understanding. But I have been forever changed in His Presence and will offer all that I am in His service.

Mercy Flow

Mercy flow so sweetly down
upon my lovesick heart.
Wash away all fear and shame,
God's grace to me impart.

Love of God come fill my soul
with peace to conquer strife.
Consume my heart with joy sublime
and God's Abundant Life.

Blood of Christ, so pure and strong
rush freely through my veins.
Cleanse every place inside of me
'til only Christ remains.

Lord, my God, to You I cry!
You are my all in all.
Come breathe in me Your very Life,
upon Your grace I fall.

To Know God

The Lord God is the Eternal, Almighty God, and He is infinitely beyond human comprehension. Majestic in power, radiant in beauty, He "alone is immortal and lives in unapproachable light." Though His glory and nature are most certainly evidenced by His wondrous creation, He Himself cannot be known save through a divine revelation. To be sure, the human mind can be filled with *knowledge about* the Divine Creator, but true *intimate knowledge* of Him can never be attained through cognitive effort, as noble as this effort may be. Striving with the mind to know this God is akin to a two-year-old child attempting to analyze and understand theories of quantum physics! "Oh, the depths of the riches of the wisdom and knowledge of God! How unsearchable are His judgements...Who has known the mind of the Lord?" However, when we seek Him out through another path—that of God's Spirit—we arrive at a blessed discovery: He is ready to make Himself known! For He tells us that, through a divine revelation, we can indeed come to know the incomprehensible God! The elusive doorway to deep knowledge of God is found not through intellectual prowess, but through child like faith. Knowing God is no complicated matter at all; rather, it is as simple as "Jesus loves me, this I know, for the Bible tells me so!" Moved by His ferocious love for you and me, this God became a Man and gave Himself unto death on a rugged cross to pave the way for this divine revelation to fill our hearts.

Risen from the dead, the beautiful Savior beckons us, "Behold, I stand at the door and knock. If anyone hears my voice and opens the door, I will come in and commune with him, and he with Me." Can you hear Him wooing you to a deep place of intimacy with Himself? Can you feel the vibrations of His violent love as He calls you beyond your mind's capacity to know Him into a realm of rich, Life-sustaining communion? "And By [God's Spirit] we cry, 'Abba, Father!'" Let us cease striving in the flesh and begin to allow God's Spirit to move us to the place where "deep calls unto deep", forging intimate bonds between child and Father. O, to enter the Most Holy Place and experience Spirit-born intimacy with the King of kings and Lord of lords! May this be the longing of our hearts and the sole passion of our lives!

Consume Me

Father so holy and pure, may Your glorious Face shine brilliantly upon me, clothing me in the garments of Your grace. Let the fire of Your divine love consume my heart, that I may show forth accurately the light of this love to a lost and dying world. O, Lord, that Your Spirit would stir in me those rivers of living water and, as a fountain, flush them through the very pores of my life! Would that I were afloat on the sea of Your divine peace, basking in the very Presence of the Lord my God! Yes, your peace is truly beyond measure, your rest beyond understanding!

O, Divine One, blow Your sweet breath of life upon the garden of my soul, bringing refreshment and strength to weary, stagnant places deep within. Fill to overflowing this vessel of Yours, O Lord, and make of me exactly who You want me to be!

I am Yours

I have to You, O Lord, eternally acquiesced
all that I am and all that I have,
for You are my soul's rest.

Before Your throne I humbly and gratefully bow,
as with love and compassion I ne'er have known
You crown my weary brow.

And as the Glory and Lifter of my head,
You raise me up and encourage my heart,
"By Me, son, You'll be led."

Now lead me, Lord, to heights beyond my sight!
I am Yours and You are mine,
Together, let's take flight!

Words Cannot Express

Where are the words to express adequately what You mean to me, wonderful God? Had I at my disposal even the most descriptive and beautiful words in existence, the use of these would still leave me dissatisfied in the end. For You are truly indescribable, and with every stroke of the pen I become more acutely aware of my inability to express to You in writing what are the rhythms of my heartbeat. So, gracious God, I beseech you to listen to my heart as it throbs with desire to love you. What my pen cannot sufficiently express to You, allow the life I live before You to proclaim fully: that You are everything to me, Father. Thank You for Your unfailing, unconditional, everlasting love—this love that has both conquered and empowered me, both broken me and raised me to Life! Let the same be the very definition of my life, as You form Yourself in me! Yes, Lord Jesus, as a river so strong, flow this love through me to others, that they too may be captured by You!

God Over All

Christ the King, emanating wave after wave of glory from His majestic Presence, calls to His creation. He commands the stars above and seas beneath, and they genuflect at the very Word of His mouth, for He is God. Beside Him there is no other, and through Him the universe is sustained, receiving its very existence from His pleasurable will. And though galaxies tremble before Him in reverence and mountains bow at His feet, there remains a force yet to be fully conquered by this God: the will of the human heart. For in His great desire to commune intimately with His most beloved creature, He has imparted to mankind a most valuable and risky gift, that of free will. And sadly some have chosen not to bow their hearts before their Creator, nor to embrace sweet fellowship with Him through Jesus Christ. To be sure, one Day these hearts *will bow* before the One True God, their tongues loudly proclaiming His Lordship, only then to be thrust into an eternity of unspeakable agony! For by then, it will be too late, and these precious souls will be forever lost. And for those of us who do choose to worship the Son of God before that great and terrible Day, let us revel in the privilege of allowing the God Who reigns supremely over creation to reign supremely in our hearts! O, what an honor it is to be able to join our voices and lives with the song of the ages, as the heavens and earth declare, "Worthy is the Lamb Who was slain"! So let us not take this lightly; rather, let us walk in humility and gratefulness before our merciful King. Furthermore, may we have the passion of God burning in our hearts, motivating us to draw to Him those who have yet to yield to His amazing grace!

Encounter with God

Beholding glory as it radiates forth from His throne,
I stand motionless while it permeates skies above.
With muscles frozen and heart racing, I cry
to know this God. "Holy Lord, here's my love!"

His response echoes upon glory-filled waves of air,
"And here is Mine, son," and He shows me scars so deep.
"My love for you compelled Me to give myself unto death,
that in meadows of green with Me you might forever leap."

Through broken speech due to wondrous awe, I declare
my deep gratitude. "Yes, Lord! I long to dance with You,
to feel the warmth of this glory bathing me forever.
Basking in this love so full—this is all I long to do!

John 3:16

"For God so loved the world, that He gave His only begotten Son…" You know the rest, I am quite sure. Do these words pierce you, arousing vivid images of delight deep within your heart, or do they bounce off you with stale familiarity? When is the last time you intentionally opened the doors of your spirit to the One who "so loved you", allowing Him to awaken you once again to the awe-striking wonder of His infinite glory? His mercy toward you is utterly new each day and His love for you knows no bounds! If you are feeling that your life has become a cycle of humdrum activities interspersed with a few bland religious traditions, catch a glimpse of Jesus of Nazareth and be swept off your feet by His breath-taking love! Allow the eyes of your soul to gaze upon the risen Savior, for in so doing you will find that those all-too familiar words will spring to life, forever branding the white hot love of Christ upon the depths of your being!

Flow in Me

O Lord, Your Life is to mine as roots are to a tree, providing me with the very sustenance I need for survival as well as for growth. So let Your life-sustaining power and grace continually flow richly in me, O Lord, as I seek Your lovely face. Lord, may the sweet aroma of Your Presence fill my soul, renewing me deep within. I am refreshed, Father, as you permeate my life with the fragrance of Your Son Jesus, the Rose of Sharon. My heart's yearning is that, wherever I go, I may exude this intoxicating fragrance to those around me, drawing them to the irresistible Savior. Erode away from my life all that hinders the river of Your glory from rushing freely through me, that I may realize to its fullness the abundant life you have in store for me.

Salvation

Falling down, down into a chasm so deep,
rolling, tumbling beyond, longing to climb the steep
and daunting slope! But faster I descend as moments go by,
closer and closer to endless death do I feel. O to fly
to the top of the mount, but alas! For me-no hope!
I am doomed to fall! I shall ne'er see the top of the slope!

Then somewhere in the night so black, a voice I hear
calling to me, beckoning in tones that drown out fear.
Somehow I know this surprising voice that speaks,
and I sense its hot pursuit-that I am what it seeks!
Words protruding forth from this Mysterious One
tell of love so pure and hope of life found in God's only Son.

"Call to me, my precious child, and I shall rescue you.
and carry you e'en far beyond the elusive mountain view.
For I am the Lord your God, burning with Love's cry
to soar with you to other worlds, always with you to fly!
The recompense for sin is death, the price you surely owe,
but in your place I gladly stood and to My death did go."

My God! My Lord! Can it be that You would in my stead
die a guilty sinner's death? For me Your blood You shed?
Yet somehow in my heart of hearts I know You are the One
to save me from this dreaded fall. Who but God the Son
could fill me with such love divine and carry in His arms
my soul forevermore, to rest, secure from all alarms?

Flying up, up into a sky so blue,
Climbing, soaring above, reveling in His love so true
and ever strong. Yea, faster I ascend as moments go by,
closer and closer to endless Life I feel. O how I fly
o'er the top of the mount, and alas! For me-such hope!
I am destined to fly! In Christ I e'er soar beyond the top of the
slope!

All in All

Star of the Morn, in splendor arrayed,
through me brightly shine!
May Your glory be displayed
upon this life of mine!

King of my heart, so pure and true,
reign supremely o'er my days!
Mold me, shape me, 'til you're through;
my hands to You I raise!

Shepherd of the flock, my guide,
upon You I depend.
In You all my fears subside,
Sweet peace to me You send!

As Resurrection and as Life,
You give to me new breath.
And as You conquer sin and strife,
You bring my soul from death!

Son of Man, with humble heart
You wash my sin-stained feet.
Now to me Your grace impart,
this work in me complete.

Son of God, Almighty One,
there is no god like You.
For who above or 'neath the sun
does what You dare to do!

God of life, my all in all,
forever in me live.
At Your feet I humbly fall,
My heart to You I give!

God in Me

As light of day quietly surrenders to dark of night,
Thoughts deep within do churn. They take flight
and whisk me away to lands beyond the veil. I see
the face of Him Who sustains my soul. I'm free!
For His life, dripping with holy love and dew so sweet
stirs in me, arousing joy sublime. My heart He does complete!

But now, what's this! He calls me back to the night!
Must I depart from this Presence so lovely? I fight
against the return, objecting that I was meant for such bliss!
"Dear child, take heart, My Presence you shall not miss.
For I in you shall always be, fear not what lay in store.
Remember that I've made your heart My home forevermore!"

I Come to You

Lord God of Hosts, Almighty King, I come to You this day.
I long to open up my heart, please be my hope and stay!

Upon You shall I e'er depend, Lord God so rich in love,
for from Your hand flows mercy true, provision from above!

And when this life so harshly stings, to You my heart will run.
For You alone, my Jesus Christ, are God the Healing One!

Now from this moment forth, my God, please ever flow in me,
that others may to You be drawn, Your glory may they see!

Galatians 2:20

Crucified with Christ, my life is no longer my own to do with as I deem appropriate. Rather, this Christ has, through His brutal death upon Calvary's cross, rightfully gained full access to the throne of my life. By way of said death, the Lord Jesus has purchased me from my mortal enemy, Satan, forever redeemed me from sin, and reconciled me to the Father. Thus, my life belongs to God forever, and I surrender to Him accordingly. And this is no reluctant surrender of which I speak. He has not forced me to do anything, for such would produce only half-hearted and meaningless service. On the contrary, I am captured by a God Who would give His own Life to save me, and I freely and completely offer myself to Him. In so doing, I open up all that I am to the fullness of God's Spirit and the Lordship of His risen Son. Forever a bondservant of my Savior Jesus Christ, I am His property, and His desire is my command. And because of His deep love for me, He has chosen also to call me to His side in a love relationship. Therefore, not only am I called to serve Him for eternity as His possession, but I am also invited to walk with Him intimately as His friend. Such is the lot of him who entrusts his life into the almighty, nail-pierced hands of the Savior. Let us, without inhibition, offer ourselves to this Jesus today and discover again what it really means to be crucified with Christ and to experience the fullness of life that resides therein!

Lend Me a Song

Lend me now a song, O God, a melody for my King,
one that fully bespeaks my love, to Your Name praise I bring!
Grant me, Lord, a verse to write, a verse to match my heart,
one that truly tells of all the joy that You impart!

Stoke in me the fire of God, the coals of which burn strong!
And fill me with Your zealous love, to last the ages long!
Stir in me Your passion, Lord, for those who do not know,
that they may see Your goodness, too. Please let Your river flow!

Psalm 19

Nature declares the glory of God,
His Presence fills the earth.
From depths below to heights above,
it proclaims His endless worth.

Billowing clouds speak of fullness in God,
abundance in Christ the King.
Rain pouring down from clouds so soft
tell of Spirit outpouring.

Mountains whose crown is snow so pure
tell of heights that steal my breath.
And no greater height hath any man known
Than the Love that conquered death!

Seas whose depths are without end,
whose lengths are just the same,
cause thoughts of God to fill my heart,
for such is His great fame!

As all creation sings to You,
My Lord, my God, my King!
May my life resound as well,
let all Your praises ring!

God's Call

I sat and watched as Life moved by
and wondered in my heart.
Am I to walk or run or fly?
And how am I to start?

Because I know not what to do,
I'll just enjoy the show.
As Life moves by—O what a view!
This way, no trial or foe!

Just then, as a flash of light
might streak across the sky,
the Author came before my sight
and loved me with a sigh.

"O, my child, my precious one,
I want to speak to you.
You are my joy, my tender son,
and I've much for you to do.

A player on my stage you'll be
to seek and save the lost,
to set the dying captive free,
no matter what the cost!

And though you will have trial and foe,
on me You will depend.
My grace upon you I'll bestow
to keep you to the end.

Now's the time to enter in;
This Life you're meant to LIVE!
For as I died to conquer sin,
So shall your all you give!"

I know at last what I must do!
I'll jump into the fray!
With plaguing fears and doubts I'm through;
My life is Yours today!

Dance of the Ages

As the Lord of glory carried the weight of the ages upon His shoulders, His thoughts were fixed upon you. Held fast to that rugged cross by nails of holy love, this gracious Savior foresaw the day when He and you would dance upon the skies together, as heavenly Bridegroom and beloved Bride. And His final words, "It is finished", though spoken at death's door, were words His heart had longed to hear! For this door was but the entry way into the eternal dance hall in which He would forever dance with you! Aroused by Father's voice, Jesus the King emerged victoriously from the grave and now stands ready to claim that for which He paid such a dear price—your hand in holy matrimony! Will you say "Yes" to Him today and throw wide the gates of your soul to its radiant Lover? Do you hear the rumblings of His heart as it pounds for you with passionate desire? Surrender to Him today, and allow Him to lead you forever in the dance of the ages!

Lamb of God

Behold, the Lamb of God, seated upon the throne! Once for sinners slain, He is now risen from the dead, reigning forever in power and glory! Do you see this glorious Lamb sitting at the right hand of the Father? He is the Lamb of God Who takes away the sin of the world. Have you opened up your life to this precious, almighty Lamb, that His shed blood may flow in you, taking away all *your* sin? O, to be absolutely covered by the pure and powerful blood that washes me until I am as white as snow! There is no blood that compares to this blood, tender child of God! For it is a continuously flowing fountain of cleansing and redemption for those who would venture under its deluge. Won't you be bathed today in the richness of the Lamb's blood?

The Good Shepherd

Jesus Christ, the Good Shepherd, longs to lead you "beside quiet waters" and "in paths of righteousness for His Name's sake." As a sheep relies upon its shepherd for everything it needs, so the Lord's desire is that you would allow Him to be your all in all. He longs to be there as the answer to every problem you encounter. When you feel as though the circumstances and trials of life have caused you to lose your way on the journey, look to Jesus your Shepherd, for He will serve as your faithful guide, steering you in the right direction. When you find yourself in lack, you will discover Him to be an all-sufficient Provider, meeting every need you have. When you feel the enemy pressing upon you from every side, the Lord will be your strong protector. As He promised in His Word, you will find your refuge in the shadow of His wings. So if you are a sheep who is in need today, gaze into the eyes of the Good Shepherd, and bask in the warmth of His unconditional love for you. Then allow Him to reveal this love to you in the form of guidance, provision, and protection.

The Way, the Truth, and the Life

The Lord Jesus boldly declared, "I am the Way, the Truth, and the Life. No one comes unto the Father except through Me." In making this proclamation, the Savior was imparting divine revelation: that He, as the Messiah, is *the only way* to God. O, do you know this Messiah? Have you accepted His welcome invitation to enter through Him into the heart of the Father of all creation and the Creator of your life? His voice speaks to you today, calling you unto Himself, pleading with you to forsake any notion that there might be some other way to absolute truth and abundant life other than Himself! "My child, would I have shed my precious blood, dying a brutal death upon a cross, if there had been another way to save you? So please accept the free gift that I offer you and fully embrace the eternal life and truth that await you through the doors of My cross!" Do you hear His voice as He wins your heart with sweet whispers of freedom? As He says elsewhere in His Word, "you shall know the truth, and the truth shall set you free!" The ultimate Truth is Jesus Christ Himself, and He longs to set you free from any shackles and chains that may bind you. So diligently seek His face, that you may indeed know Him, and thus be set free! And, as the very definition of Life itself, this beautiful Son of God deeply desires to be your very life! In Him is the overflowing abundance of Life for which you were created. Why not wholeheartedly embrace this merciful King in order that His fullness may flow in and through you!

The Light of the World

"The light shines in the darkness, and the darkness has not overcome it." We need this light to shine in our darkened world, so that we may live in the realms of beauty and purity the Lord has prepared for His children. The Lord Jesus said, "I am the Light of the world. Anyone who follows me will never walk in darkness." Are we in step with our King today, following closely behind His lead? For He is the Light that will defeat any darkness that my try to creep its way into our lives. O, to experience the darkness-conquering Light of the Father, as He continually fills our lives with a revelation of His Son! May the cry of our hearts be one of desire for the light of His Presence to fill our souls, that His light may shine from within, defeating all darkness that threatens from without. Let us surrender all to this glorious Light today and experience the eternal victory and freedom He brings!

The Resurrection and the Life

Do you fear death and what lays beyond the grave, precious child of the King? Do you wonder where you may spend eternity or whether or not you have what it takes to make it to Heaven? Well, there is good news flowing from the lips of our Lord Jesus: "I am the Resurrection and the Life. He who believes in Me will live, even though he dies." Hallelujah! Yes, if you have the Lord Jesus Christ today, reigning in your heart as almighty God and Savior, then you have what it takes to "make it" to Heaven! The Lord has conquered death and hell, so if you fear either of these, why not allow God's Spirit to deposit deep, blessed assurance in your inner being today? Simply throw your life and eternal destiny upon this risen Lord Jesus, and allow Him to forever be your Resurrection and your Life!

Love Comes Forth

Love comes forth, riding waves of victory
to capture my heart that now belongs to Him!
And capture me Love does with such glee,
as joy over me does fill His heart to its brim.

Caught up into the everlasting arms of Love,
I feel the wind of His victory underneath,
as it carries us to worlds beyond and above!
O, how my heart hangs upon His as a wreath!

Had I known this Love to be so glorious,
I ne'er would have lived without!
For now that I feel this Love Victorious,
I shall forever ride with Him, no doubt!

The Silhouette

Set against the backdrop of a pale blue sky is a silhouette that captures my undivided attention. At first glance I thought it to be only a figment of my imagination, but through squinted eyes I began to make out this figure, and I realized this to be no dream at all. On the contrary, I see before me an unmistakable image of the risen Lord Jesus! Sitting gloriously upon a steed, He appears as if He is ready to charge forward with great purpose. I see pupils consumed with flames of fire as they gaze upon the earth. I can almost feel the wings of the wind ruffling in anticipation of His movement. Then I am captured by divine revelation from His heart, as if I know what are the very thoughts therein. His eyes are a window to the depths of His being, expressing the burning desire within His heart for intimacy with His bride! Yes, He is awaiting your cry, precious creature of God! He yearns to hear you call His Name, as this call will release Him in His fullness to soar down upon the wings of the wind and rescue you. It will release Him to charge into the depths of your heart and make His eternal home within its walls. O, how His heart longs for intimate communion with yours! Do you sense this raging desire in the Lord's heart as it protrudes from His glorified body, permeating the sky? Simply call upon the Name of this Rider, Jesus Christ, surrendering all to Him, and He will ride into the center of your life, consuming you with His love and taking you on the adventure of a lifetime!

That Day

Face to face with the One Whose very Presence causes nations to tremble, I stand before my Maker on that Day, unable to speak. All the excuses in the world fade to nothing in the light of this glorious God. Every thought, deed, and word of my life is laid bare before His terrible holiness, stripping me of any illusions of my worthiness even to be before Him, let alone to enter into His heavenly sanctuary for all eternity! Then, He tenderly reaches out His almighty hand and touches me, driving all fear from my heart. "Son, I love you. Your sins and mistakes are many in number and great in magnitude, but they pale in comparison to My love for you. My Son Jesus shed His blood for you, and because you placed your entire life in His hands, trusting Him to save you and surrendering to His Lordship, you are cleansed by this blood. My heart weeps over your sin, but it rejoices to be able to declare you to be 'not guilty' by virtue of the sufficiency of My Son's sacrifice in your behalf! The price has been paid in full, so enter now into the joy of your Lord to enjoy eternity upon eternity of unadulterated intimacy with Me!"

The tears that begin to stream down my face are tears of both joy and grief. I am obviously overjoyed at the goodness of the Lord. But I am also deeply sorrowful for all the times in my life that I used this unconditional love to do what I wanted to do. O, to have those moments back that I might deny myself, choosing that which would please this amazing Lover of my soul! But thanks be to God for His eternal grace and mercy!

Lord God Most High

Lord God Most High, You are exalted above all creation, gloriously filling eternity with Your indescribable majesty! My heart revels in the unspeakable beauty of Your holy Presence! From everlasting to everlasting, You are God. Creatures in heav'n above and on earth below humbly worship before Your throne, Father. With but a breath You create worlds anew, all of whom yearn with desire to adore You! Creation is sustained by the power of Your spoken Word, Lord of hosts, so please grant me the honor of hearing Your irresistible voice, my King! O, You who permeates the universe with glory divine, consume my desperate heart with radiant beams of Your splendor! Lord Jesus, my soul is overwhelmed that You Who command the heavens would condescend to love me with such tenderness. Had I not been transfixed by the sight and thought of You, I would have fled, for fear that this love was but a dream too amazing to be true! My Lord, thank You for stopping me in my tracks with Your stunning radiance, for You have absolutely convinced me that Your love is indeed a reality, and have thus forever captured my heart! Hallelujah! Honor and praise be unto Your Name forever, my God, for You alone are worthy of glory! Mighty One of Israel, exploit any areas in my life that are not fully conquered by Your sovereignty. Then, in Your great kindness, firmly establish Your supreme authority over these areas, that my entire being may be in perfect step with Your will. Yes, Lord God, allow Your preeminence over creation to fully manifest itself in the very depths of my heart!

Before the Throne

Glory drips from Your holy throne
as water from melting ice.
And those beholding long and groan,
their hearts by You enticed.

As no exception to the rule,
my heart does skip a beat
and does receive eternal fuel
when fall I at Your feet.

This fuel, Your love—how strong and true—
so graciously imparts
a joy that turns gray skies to blue,
a fire deep in my heart!

O, joy sublime and fire so bright,
unhindered through me, shine!
That others may come to the Light,
flow through me love divine!

And when they come, Lord, to Your grace
so rich and full and free,
allow them to behold Your face—
hear now, my humble plea!

Born to Fly

Is life a struggle that you simply cannot seem to overcome, one in which your days are dominated by weariness and strife? Do you feel as if you will never see the light at the end of the tunnel, sometimes wondering why you are even on this earth? If so, the answer rests in the Lord Jesus Christ, the Maker heaven and earth. His Word declares that "those who wait upon the Lord shall renew their strength. They shall rise up with wings as an eagle!" Let this be as music to your ears, dear creature of the one true God—in the Lord, you will fly! You were not born to struggle through life, barely making it through each day, dreading the next! On the contrary, you were born to soar as the eagle soars! If you wait upon Your Maker, opening up the depths of Your soul to His touch, He will infuse you with power divine, causing you to take flight in Him! He longs for you to have a revelation of who you become when you are born from above—born of His Spirit. You become an heir of God Himself and a joint-heir with the Son of God, Jesus Christ! This means you are royalty and, accordingly, are to live "the good life" in the Spirit. For princes and princesses do not simply scrape by on crumbs; rather, they live off the fat of the land! The same applies for you in the Spirit, if you are redeemed by the blood of the Lamb! You are "more than a conqueror through Him Who loved you" and have the authority to walk on water as Peter did! When you fully tap in to the divine Life residing in your spirit, a new power is in operation—"the Spirit of life in

Christ Jesus"! Through His Spirit of life, you can live a supernatural life! You can "trample on snakes and scorpions" and demolish strongholds in the Spirit, "casting down vain imaginations and anything that would exalt itself against the knowledge of God"! Does flying in the Lord equate with no trial or tribulation? By no means! In fact the Lord promised that in this world we would have tribulation, and in James' letter, the Lord admonishes us to "count it all joy when you face trials of many kinds"! So flight in the Lord does not mean sailing through life with no trials to come your way. Rather, it means that you live from an eternal perspective *in the midst of* the trials, considering them as "light and momentary afflictions"! To fly in the Lord is to live in the realm in which God lives, thus embracing trial, knowing it can only serve to elevate your flight to an even higher level in Him! This higher life has nothing to do with circumstance and everything to do with revelation of your position in Christ. Paul said, "I have learned the secret of being content in any and every situation…I can do all things through Christ Who strengthens me"! So let us open up our hearts to Holy Spirit revelation of who we are in Christ, casting aside fear and anxiety, and let us be caught up into the glory of the Lord. For as we live in the realm of His glory and His love, we will truly fly as the eagle flies and be conformed into His very likeness!

II Corinthians 4:6

"For God made His light shine in our hearts to give us the light of the knowledge of the glory of God in the face of Christ." Do you see the face of the Lord Jesus today, radiating the very glory of God from deep within your heart? His face is full of beauty beyond compare, beauty to consume your soul with adoration of Him. O, to gaze upon the wonderful face of the Master! His face is full of compassion, shedding a tear as you grieve during a time of loss, as He is the Man of sorrows. His face is full of purpose, speaking words of hope and encouragement when you are discouraged. Do you hear Him speaking softly to Your soul of its worth and value in Him? His face beams with joy at the very notion of intimate relationship with you! Simply lift the eyes of your spirit to look upon His lovely face, and discover that His unparalleled joy will be your strength and your song! Never has there been nor ever will there be a face like that of this King, one that with one glance can both set the soul at rest and cause it to soar!

Divine Consecration

Spirit of God, kindle deep within my soul the unquenchable fire of God, that I may brightly burn with love divine. Set me ablaze with unbridled passion for my Savior, Jesus Christ. Make of me a holy sacrifice and lay me upon the altar of my Father, that all the dross of my life might be fully consumed by Your holy flame. Through Your refining process, forge me into the man you would have me to be, that I may be totally consecrated unto Father's purposes. O, how I long for others to mistake me for my glorious Savior Jesus Christ, as You increasingly form me into His likeness. Yes, Lord, let the beatings of Your heart overtake those of mine until the two become one, and Your divine desires are finding their fulfillment through the avenue of my life! Conform me, almighty Potter, into Your very image, that others may see Your matchless glory abiding in and pouring through me!

Deep Stirrings

Volcanic stirrings deep within,
consuming fire blazes!
Burning chaff and cleansing sin,
my spirit God's touch raises!

This fire so strong in my soul burns,
its kindling, Christ the Lord!
My desperate heart with longing yearns
for God, the One adored!

Through fullness of my God and King,
I soar beyond the sky!
To me the pearls of Heav'n to bring
This King did bleed and die!

These pearls now resting in my heart
ride deep volcanic streams.
And in me they God's grace impart,
so through me His love beams!

Forever

Forever to rest in His strong arms,
would I give all I have!
E'er safe from would-be harms,
He for past wounds is salve.

O, this precious Christ of mine,
how He fills my desire!
Yea, I with Him always shall dine,
Ne'er of His food to tire!

This food, to do His pleasing will,
is to my soul a treat.
In Him my heart feels such a thrill,
His pleasure, its very beat.

Other joys do quickly fade
in light of my great Lord!
Forever I shall with Him stay,
His beauty to adore!

Psalm 93

"The seas have lifted up, O Lord, the seas have lifted up their voice; the seas have lifted up their pounding waves…" Waves of trial are pounding upon the shores of your life, slowly eroding the will and desire to continue. Your hope in the Lord is gradually waning and being replaced by despair of life itself. You wonder why He has not rescued you from the relentless clutches of Trial's deadly grip. "…*Mightier* than the thunder of the great waters, *mightier* than the breakers of the sea—the Lord on high is mighty!" Lift your eyes to gaze beyond the breaking waves to see the risen Lord Jesus reigning in victory over all that would threaten to devour you! Do you see the fire of love burning in His merciful eyes? Allow these eyes to pierce you to the very depths of Your soul, infusing you with revelation knowledge that you are more than a conqueror through Him! Hear His voice that drowns out that of the waves, as He encourages your battered and weathered soul, "In this world you will have tribulation. But take heart! I have overcome the world!" Faith is born through receiving the unbroken Word of Christ, so allow His resounding voice to impart to you mountain-moving faith, dear child of God! By virtue of His death and resurrection, Christ has forever crushed the enemy under His feet! And, if you have surrendered to His Lordship, you are *in* this victorious Christ. Thus, in Christ, you have also overcome the world! So see this mighty God exalted high above the dreaded waves and hear His voice as it overwhelms their pounding, that Trial's deadly grip might give way to Hope's loving grasp.

Your Presence

In Your intoxicating Presence, O Lord, I am filled with a joy that far surpasses any that I have ever known! You are the Lord God Who consumes my heart with a joy that is unspeakably wonderful and replete with glory! Your unparalleled joy is the very strength of my heart, imparting to the depths of my being supernatural power to rise up amid the adversities I face. O, this house of flesh simply cannot contain the fullness of joy with which Your Spirit fills me! I feel as though I were a hydrant of water that, when burst open, gushes out with massive force! For so is this joy that resides inside of me, rushing forth in rivers of living water as You burst me open with Your heavenly touch! These rivers are the manifestation of Your glory as You so graciously stimulate my soul and flow Yourself through my life to others! I long, my Lord, for these rivers of glory to gush forth through the power of Your Holy Spirit, inundating this land until the knowledge of Your wonderful Presence fills the earth! Lord, consume Your people with Your holy joy and powerfully manifest Your glory in and through us, that Your Kingdom may be fully established in the earth!

Ecstasy

Western sky, so deep and blue
does boast a lovely prize.
Transfixed, I sit and gaze into
this rider of the skies.

For as my eyes now fall upon
this bright and setting sun,
I see it to be but the pawn
in service to God's Son!

Instantly I feel His rush,
the ecstasy of love!
My soul is captured by His gush
of glory from above!

He speaks to me of Life beyond
the humdrum of the day.
He vows to give this vagabond
a heav'nly place to stay!

He spreads His arms across the sky,
revealing hands so scarred.
"My love for you," I hear Him cry,
"is fierce and without guard!"

And in reply, I vow to Him
my heart, my love, my all!
"O King of kings, highest heaven's Gem,
Here at Your feet I fall!"

This high within is like no drug
which e'er I have known!
Be still, my heart! O, how His tug
does make you flesh from stone!

As I waken from the trance,
I fear 'twas merely a dream!
But then I see the sky's expanse;
I feel the sun's pure gleam!

And God reminds me of His touch,
So tender and so true!
"Abounding love and grace as much
shall always follow you!"

God of Glory

God of glory, Sovereign of the universe, You are beyond compare! Unlimited in power and grace, You are the Superlative of all creation! Descend now upon the winds of Your breath in the earth and reveal that which is otherwise unknown: love divine. Then allow the blood-soaked wings of this love to expand fully within me, causing me to take flight in Christ the King! May this love, mingled with Your mercy so pure, flood the depths of my soul with the sweet aroma of holy purpose. Impart to me zealous passion dripping with sacred destiny as You breathe Your breath of love into my longing heart! O sovereign Master of life, come establish the governmental authority of Your blessed Kingdom within the domain of *my* life, that I a tabernacle of Your ceaseless praise might be! O Rock of ages, my very existence is founded upon You and, as Israel of old, does receive from You its fresh and living water! Rock within me, flow now Your living water of love through the pipeline of my life, that others may drink of its richness and be drawn to its Source, the God of glory!

Rest in God

Lord of Hosts, You are overflowing with power and girded with strength! Creation trembles before Your awesome Presence as You boldly move in the earth to accomplish Your purposes. Majestic Warrior, You invite me to rest in Your arms so strong—Your arms of Love that hung upon Calvary's tree. O, how my heart longs to accept Your holy invitation, for in this divine rest I discover not only peace and joy beyond comprehension, but also victory over the enemy of my soul. Yes, Lord, sweet deliverance manifests not through my valiant efforts, but through Your mighty Spirit, as you conquer my adversary with but a breath from Your holy nostrils. Reigning King of my heart, awaken my soul to sing of the wondrous works of my Savior! As I rest in You, may Your tender rescue move my heart to absolute adoration of my glorious God! As You lead forth the armies of heaven to vanquish the foe, let me ever in You be found, obediently marching to the beat of Your drum! O Victor of the ages, defeat the wavering desires and distractions that attempt to thwart my God-breathed resolve to follow hard after You! By Your grace, allow the rest I experience in You to produce fruit in keeping with Spirit-bred transformation. And when on the Last Day I throw myself at Your feet, all my crowns humbly offering to You, may words protruding forth from You be those that my ears were made to hear, "Well done, good and faithful servant! Enter now into the joy of Your Lord!"

Jesus the Lord

Who is this Man I see before me, from Whom the darkness flees? His light so brilliant, yet so soft, defeats death and imparts life, God's glory to reveal. What Love is this that beckons even me, the one who shouted in turn, "Crucify!" — the one who scorned His brutal sacrifice? Who is this God so pure and strong—Whose victory o'er the grave now wrought— Who looks at me with piercing eyes and loves me to my soul's depths? I feel as though my heart will melt within me as with one glance He violently loves me, shaking me at the core of my being! "I am Jesus the Lord, great God and Savior of all, and I shine forth as light of the world, hope of the ages. I died and rose again that I might shine my light brightly from within you, my child, and that I might be in you the eternal hope of glory! So open up your heart and life to the fullness of my reign, and discover that my Presence inside of you will explode within, manifesting glorious abundance of life!" As if my heart had been created for this instant, without hesitation it cries, "Yes, O Lord, I throw open my life to You that You might in all Your glory rule every facet of my being! As light of the world, shine from within the depths of my heart, bringing darkness to its knees. And as hope of the ages, carry me upon the wings of Your zealous love, that all in our path might be caught up into the eternal hope found in You!"

Rescued

Beset by foes on every side, I call upon the Lord!
He flies with fierce and holy zeal to rescue and to pour
His love on me-I feel His touch! My heart is His alone,
For when my life seemed at its end, He on me His light shone!

Consumed with burning love for Him, I am God's-no doubt!
Now I His high and lofty praise in all the earth must shout
Til every creature in the world before Him humbly falls—
Til every tribe and tongue upon the Name of Jesus calls!

So Lord, anoint my lips to speak and from me overflow
That I may Your great story tell and Your love ever show!
And let my life a canvas be upon which is displayed
The beauty of my Lord and God-in majesty arrayed!

How Much More

Richly bestowing unspeakably wonderful gifts upon His children, your God is a "how much more" kind of God! He declares in His Word, "...if many died by [Adam'] sin, *how much more* did God's grace and the gift that came by the grace of the one man, Jesus Christ, overflow to the many!...if, by [Adam's] sin, death reigned through him, *how much more* will those who receive God's abundant provision of grace and of the gift of righteousness reign in life through the one man, Jesus Christ!" Because you descend from the first man, Adam, you are born into sin and are therefore under condemnation because of his sin in the garden of Eden. But the glorious God, the amazing Savior Jesus Christ, made abundant provision for you and for me through His death and resurrection. If you have flung wide the gates of your heart and embraced the Lamb of God in all His fullness, you qualify for God's free gift of righteousness. If you have invited King Jesus to establish within you His supreme Lordship and to cleanse You by His blood, then you are "a brand new creation; old things have passed away and all things have become new!" You are not bound to live under the dominion of Adam's curse; rather, God the Son has paved the way for you to soar on wings as an eagle! You are destined to reign in life through Christ Your Lord, weary child of God! He has much more for you than mere existence—He has in store for you overwhelming abundance and overcoming victory! If you are worn thin from endless cycles of failure and repentance, simply come to Your Savior. "Come to me, all who are weary and heavy laden, and I will give you rest. Take my yoke upon you and learn from Me, for I am gentle and humble in heart, and you will find rest for your souls. For my yoke is easy and My burden is light." Do you hear Him wooing you to a life of rest in Him? Do you sense His gentle call to surrender control of your life to Him? As you acquiesce unto the Lord, you will joyfully discover His power to be "sufficient for you, for [His] power is made perfect in [your] weakness!" And as you allow His glorious, mountain-moving strength to well up within you, your feet will tread on water, as Peter of long ago, and your life will be transformed into the very likeness of the Son of God! If this amazing God shed His own blood for you while you were rebellious and lost in your sins, *how much more* will His abounding love and grace cause you to triumph in life when you have turned your heart over to Him in full surrender! So, casting aside all doubt and fear, behold now the risen Lamb of God as He extends to you an invitation to enter fully into your destiny as one who reigns with Him!

He Lives

He created.
My heart from Him received its form
And through Him had its life.
He wept.
My heart rebelled and went astray
And welcomed sin and strife.

He lives!

He descended.
Assuming flesh, He walked as man,
Constrained by holy desire.
He died.
He hung upon a rugged tree
To save me from the mire.

He lives!

He rose.
Conqu'ring death, He from the grave
Emerged, the glorious Lord!
He ascended.
To the Father's side He flew,
God's Darling, so adored!

My heart—now broken by Love so pure,
By Christ, Who depths of hell did endure—
comes to life!

He speaks.
My heart races to capture the sound,
To feel its holy vibration!
He moves.
My heart dances to rhythms of love
And flutters at the sensation!

He lives!
Thus, I live.

He comes.
My heart so widely flings its gates,
Inviting the Master in.
He consumes.
My heart so softly melts at His touch
And bids goodbye all sin!

He lives!
Thus, I live.

Now this constraint that moved His heart,
This Love that Life to me did impart,
Moves me!

Conquering Love

Conquering love flows sweetly down
From Heav'n, its wave I feel!
Pure touch of Christ the Holy One
Consumes me and does steal
My heart away! O, thorny crown,
Now to my soul reveal
Conquering love!

Living water rushes out
From Christ, my Lovely Lord!
Its streams run freely from the spout
Of Heav'n! O, let me ford
The river of Your love and shout
Of Christ, Who in me pours
Living water!

Consuming fire within me, burn!
Blaze forth and make my heart
A flame for Christ, for Whom I yearn!
My foe's attack now thwart!
O, Holy Ghost, so deftly turn
And to my soul impart
Consuming fire!

Two Thieves

Life as a cruel thief steals my dreams
Then laughs.
Christ as a beautiful thief steals my heart
Then loves.

O come and take my heart, O Lord!
I offer up my life!
And now on me Your mercy pour
To conquer sin and strife!

Blow, sweet holy wind of Christ,
Infuse me with Your breath!
By You, Lord, may I be enticed
Forever, e'en past death!

When Life as a cruel thief steals your dreams
Just laugh.
For Christ as a beautiful thief will steal your heart
Then love.

Printed in the United States
48598LVS00007B/102